My
JOURNEY IN
OBEDIENCE

My
JOURNEY IN
OBEDIENCE

SHAVON SELLERS

ISBN: 978-1-7341479-4-0 (Paperback)

Library of Congress Control Number: 2019956214

Front cover image by Prize Publishing House, LLC.
Book design by Prize Publishing House, LLC.

Printed by Prize Publishing House, LLC, in the United States of America.

First printing edition 2019.

Prize Publishing House, LLC
P.O. Box 9856
Chesapeake, VA 23321

Prize
PUBLISHING HOUSE

www.PrizePublishingHouse.com

Contents

INTRODUCTION

I pray that as you read or have read *When Obeying God Makes You Look Stupid* you are blessed and equipped to move forward to those places that God is showing you.

Never downplay the significance of your experiences. As you continue to experience life, dreams, and visions and continue in your season of transition, I encourage you to reflect on your experiences and write them down. By writing in your journal, you will find the beauty of who you really are, why you're here, and why God has chosen this path for you.

Journaling allows you to reflect upon yourself and to take a deeper dive in those things that are concerning you. You are able to write your thoughts and to pray over them daily. Your feelings, your beliefs, your lessons learned are valuable, they're important, and they're also essential in your journey.

As you journal, take a deep look within and be honest with yourself. Spend time with God daily. But most of all be open and sincere with yourself. You will begin to see how your experiences shape who you are and what you need to do to move forward. You will acknowledge those people, places, and things that are both good and bad for you. But most of all you will find yourself on your way to your destiny.

Do not be afraid of transition and do not be afraid to share what you are experiencing with others. The Bible tells us that to everything there is a season. While you may not be in your season of transition, you are either entering this season or just coming out. Wherever you may find yourself at this time, continue to trust God and be obedient to what He is showing you and saying to you.

It is my prayer that as you go on this journey of self-awareness and self-discovery, that you are empowered to push forward no matter what it looks like right now. I pray that God will reveal Himself to you during this process, and that you will gain a better understanding of who you are in Him and why He has chosen you for such a time as this. Continue to pray and press forward in this season and watch God blow your mind!

WHEN YOUR OBEDIENCE DOESN'T MAKE SENSE TO THE NATURAL EYE

"Eye hath not seen, nor ear heard, neither
have entered into the heart of man the
things which God hath prepared for them
that love Him." – 1 Corinthians 2:9

*H*ave you ever found yourself in a situation that did not quite make sense to you or make you second guess yourself? Have you ever had others to tell you that's a crazy idea? Have you ever thought to yourself, "No, that can't be right, that's crazy?" At some point in our lives, we have all found ourselves in a similar situation. Even in those times when you know that it is the Lord, it still does not make sense.

The scripture says, *"Eye hath not seen, nor ear heard, neither have entered into the heart of man the things which God hath prepared for them that love Him."* This means that our minds cannot think of nor comprehend those things that God has in store for our lives. If we cannot think it, that means that we cannot see it for it to even begin to make sense to us.

Throughout your journey, God has revealed to you some things that may have caused you to run away from Him and to ignore what He has told or shown you. You may have shared it with others who thought you were crazy, which in turn made you doubt yourself although you knew it was God who showed you.

God has prepared you for such a time and now you must make preparations for yourself. You will begin to see things and people change around you. You will have to embrace the change and know that all things are working together for a greater purpose.

When sharing what does not make sense to others, be very careful because people can often talk you right out of your blessing. It does not make sense to them so you cannot expect them to support or encourage you during this time. Therefore, it is important that you remain strong in your faith. Though, they may not understand nor agree with what you are saying, you must still plan your actions carefully and show them that you genuinely care, and that this is a God decision, not a personal decision.

Take the time to reflect on these things and make a bold decision to share your story with others. Now is the time to be honest with yourself and how you feel in moments of transition even when it does not make sense to the natural eye!

JOURNAL YOUR THOUGHTS

**What are some things that God has shown me
that I know won't make sense to others?**

_____

_____

_____

_____

_____

_____

_____

_____

_____

_____

_____

_____

_____

JOURNAL YOUR THOUGHTS

**How can sharing my story help others
and be a testament of my faith?**

_____

_____

_____

_____

_____

_____

_____

_____

_____

_____

_____

_____

_____

JOURNAL YOUR THOUGHTS

What are some signs of transition that I have noticed in my life?

_____

_____

_____

_____

_____

_____

_____

_____

_____

_____

_____

_____

_____

_____

JOURNAL YOUR THOUGHTS

Now that I recognize signs of transition, I plan to:

_____

_____

_____

_____

_____

_____

_____

_____

_____

_____

_____

_____

_____

JOURNAL YOUR THOUGHTS

How can I show people in my life that I genuinely care, even though I am in transition?

_____

_____

_____

_____

_____

_____

_____

_____

_____

_____

_____

_____

_____

JOURNAL YOUR THOUGHTS

**What are some things I can be honest about
although it may not look pretty?**

_____

_____

_____

_____

_____

_____

_____

_____

_____

_____

_____

_____

_____

TRUSTING GOD WHEN YOU CAN'T TRACE OR TRACK HIM

"Have not I commanded thee? Be strong and of a good courage; be not afraid, neither be thou dismayed: for the Lord thy God is with thee whithersoever thou goest." – Joshua 1:9

Things happen often in our lives and though we know that it is God, we do not always understand what He is doing. To us it looks like our world is coming to an end and we are experiencing the worst season of our lives. It is important to know that God has promised to be with us in ALL things and that He will never leave us nor forsake us.

When we trust God, we are letting Him know that we have confidence, faith or hope in Him. We must show Him that we trust Him by moving when He says move even when we can't track or trace Him. As we begin and continue to move, God will show Himself to us and give us assurance as we go forward, but first He must know that our trust is in Him.

<u>What the Bible Says About Trusting God:</u>

"Blessed is the man that trusteth in the Lord, and whose hope the Lord is. For he shall be as a tree planted by the waters, and that spreadeth out her roots by the river, and shall not see when heat cometh, but her leaf shall be green; and shall not be careful in the year of drought, neither shall cease from yielding fruit." – Jeremiah 17:7-8

"For we walk by faith, not by sight ." – 2 Corinthians 5:7

"The fear of man bringeth a snare: but whoso putteth his trust in the Lord shall be safe." – Proverbs 29:25

"Commit thy way unto the Lord; trust also in him; and he shall bring it to pass." – Psalm 37:5

JOURNAL YOUR THOUGHTS

In those moments where I can't track God, I feel:

_____

_____

_____

_____

_____

_____

_____

_____

_____

_____

_____

_____

_____

_____

JOURNAL YOUR THOUGHTS

What are some things that God is waiting for me to move on?

_____

_____

_____

_____

_____

_____

_____

_____

_____

_____

_____

_____

_____

JOURNAL YOUR THOUGHTS

Why do I feel God wants me to move/transition?

_____

_____

_____

_____

_____

_____

_____

_____

_____

_____

_____

_____

_____

JOURNAL YOUR THOUGHTS

What are some things I am trusting God for in this season?

_____

_____

_____

_____

_____

_____

_____

_____

_____

_____

_____

_____

JOURNAL YOUR THOUGHTS

Though I can't track God, I should trust Him because:

_____

_____

_____

_____

_____

_____

_____

_____

_____

_____

_____

_____

_____

JOURNAL YOUR THOUGHTS

What are some things I have experienced where God has shown me that I could trust Him even when I could not track Him?

_____

_____

_____

_____

_____

_____

_____

_____

_____

_____

_____

_____

_____

DEVELOP AN EAR TO HEAR THE VOICE OF THE LORD

"But without faith it is impossible to please Him: for He that cometh to God must believe that He is, and that He is a rewarder of them that diligently seek Him." – Hebrews 11:6

Knowing the voice of God in our lives is so important. Do you often ask yourself what does God sound like? Or how does God speak to you?

To know and hear the voice of God, you must first be in relationship with Him. Relationship is vital because that is where you get to know the heart of God, His desires for your life, where He would have you to go, and what He would have for you to do. Relationship means spending quality time with Him, talking to Him throughout the day, praying consistently, and reading His Word. You cannot be in relationship with someone who you do not spend time with.

You must make a personal, conscious decision to become more aware of God's instructions and to know what is the voice of God and what is not the voice of God. When it is the voice of God your spirit will be settled; it will not come attached with worry, confusion, or anxiety. You will have peace.

When you know that God speaks to you, whether it is by way of a prophetic word, dreams, visions, His Word, or in prayer, it is important to remain confident in what you know and to have someone in your circle who supports you and understands the calling that is on your life and your "crazy faith." You will know that God speaks to you and they will in turn trust the God in you.

Take some time to analyze yourself and your relationship with God and determine how you can become more aware of His voice and His instructions.

JOURNAL YOUR THOUGHTS

What are some things I can do to better recognize the voice of God?

_____

_____

_____

_____

_____

_____

_____

_____

_____

_____

_____

_____

_____

JOURNAL YOUR THOUGHTS

How and when has God spoken to me?

_____

_____

_____

_____

_____

_____

_____

_____

_____

_____

_____

_____

_____

_____

JOURNAL YOUR THOUGHTS

What does the voice of God mean to me?

_____

_____

_____

_____

_____

_____

_____

_____

_____

_____

_____

_____

_____

JOURNAL YOUR THOUGHTS

Where do I want the voice of God to lead me?

_____

_____

_____

_____

_____

_____

_____

_____

_____

_____

_____

_____

_____

JOURNAL YOUR THOUGHTS

**In times where I disobeyed the voice of
God and moved in my flesh, I felt:**

_____

_____

_____

_____

_____

_____

_____

_____

_____

_____

_____

_____

_____

_____

JOURNAL YOUR THOUGHTS

One supportive person in my circle is....
and they are supportive by:

_____

_____

_____

_____

_____

_____

_____

_____

_____

_____

_____

_____

_____

DETACHING FROM THINGS YOU ARE ATTACHED TO

*"But this one thing I do, forgetting those things
which are behind, and reaching forth unto
those things which are before, I press toward
the mark for the prize of the high calling of
God in Christ Jesus." – Philippians 3:13-14*

We all have things that we hold near and dear to our hearts. They are our life's treasures. These are things such as our spouses, children, parents, friends, church, job, house, and community. The things that we cannot imagine living without. But what happens when God tells you that you must let those things go and leave them behind? Naturally, you immediately feel a sense of loss, a sense of anxiety, and a fear of the unknown because you have never had to live without these things before. That is when your faith and trust in God must increase and be activated like never before.

You must prepare yourself mentally and emotionally before you are able to move on physically. You must process what is happening and how you are going to deal with it. You must assure yourself that everything will be okay, and that God will not lead you to a place and it is not better. Remember, God will not require you to give up something and not bless you with more than you gave up.

It is also so important to know who and what you must detach from. God will not always require that you detach from everyone and everything, so that is when you must be discerning. You must know who and what can go with you into your next season.

As you move forward in transition, think about how those people and places that you must detach from will be impacted. There will be positive and negative responses, but you have to remain steadfast and know that you are not responsible for how they respond. No matter the response, you must still press forward and detach.

When you realize that seasons change and things change, it will be easier to think about what you need to do during this time and make plans to move forward in transition.

JOURNAL YOUR THOUGHTS

What are some things I need to detach from?

_____

_____

_____

_____

_____

_____

_____

_____

_____

_____

_____

_____

_____

JOURNAL YOUR THOUGHTS

What is holding me back from detaching from things that are dear to me?

_____

_____

_____

_____

_____

_____

_____

_____

_____

_____

_____

_____

JOURNAL YOUR THOUGHTS

Why does God want me to detach from certain people and things?

_____

_____

_____

_____

_____

_____

_____

_____

_____

_____

_____

_____

_____

_____

JOURNAL YOUR THOUGHTS

How can I prepare myself to detach mentally and emotionally?

_____

_____

_____

_____

_____

_____

_____

_____

_____

_____

_____

_____

_____

JOURNAL YOUR THOUGHTS

What will I do when others don't respond to my detachment in a positive manner?

_____

_____

_____

_____

_____

_____

_____

_____

_____

_____

_____

_____

_____

JOURNAL YOUR THOUGHTS

When I must detach from things I feel:

_____

_____

_____

_____

_____

_____

_____

_____

_____

_____

_____

_____

_____

_____

OVERCOMING FEAR

*"For God hath not given us the spirit of
fear; but of power, and of love, and of
a sound mind." – 2 Timothy 1:7*

Fear is often the number one reason for not walking in the calling that God has for your life and not moving when He says move. Fear can be crippling and often a stumbling block. If you were to let fear overtake you, you would not be able to accomplish a lot of the beautiful things that you have experienced in life.

I always say that fear is false evidence appearing real. Sometimes we can talk ourselves right of a blessing because we are scared. Because we don't trust God in all things. The Word says that we should trust Him in all things, not just the small things or things that we can see and think we can control. He has given each of us the power to overcome and to make sound decisions.

A good way to overcome your fears is to activate your faith. Make that first step. As you begin to move and as God assures you along the way, you will become less fearful with each step.

You cannot listen to the enemy; instead you must stay in the Word and speak positive things over your life. Encourage yourself and stay busy with the work of the Lord so that the enemy cannot sneak in and when he does try, you are so aware of his tactics that you are able to combat.

F.E.A.R – Forget Everything and Run

Or

F.E.A.R – Face Everything and Rise

It's all in perception. Today choose to speak positive things over your life and face everything and rise.

JOURNAL YOUR THOUGHTS

My biggest fear of transition is:

_____

_____

_____

_____

_____

_____

_____

_____

_____

_____

_____

_____

_____

JOURNAL YOUR THOUGHTS

**What are some things that have been held
up in my life because of fear?**

_____

_____

_____

_____

_____

_____

_____

_____

_____

_____

_____

_____

JOURNAL YOUR THOUGHTS

When has fear caused me to override what God said?

_____

_____

_____

_____

_____

_____

_____

_____

_____

_____

_____

_____

_____

_____

JOURNAL YOUR THOUGHTS

To conquer my fears, I can:

_____

_____

_____

_____

_____

_____

_____

_____

_____

_____

_____

_____

_____

_____

JOURNAL YOUR THOUGHTS

What does God's Word say about overcoming my fears?

_____

_____

_____

_____

_____

_____

_____

_____

_____

_____

_____

_____

_____

_____

JOURNAL YOUR THOUGHTS

What can I say to myself to help overcome my fears? (Write a daily affirmation)

_____

_____

_____

_____

_____

_____

_____

_____

_____

_____

_____

_____

_____

EMBRACING THE NEW

*"Be strong and of a good courage, fear not, nor
be afraid of them: for the Lord thy God, he it
is that doth go with thee; he will not fail thee,
nor forsake thee." – Deuteronomy 31:6*

*P*eople often get excited when they think of something new.
However, when something new is something that you are
not familiar with, embracing it can be quite daunting. This
is when you must have a change in mindset.

Look at this new season as an opportunity for greatness. Think of
what you would like to experience or some things that you expect
God to do for you in this new season. Think of how this new season
and transition will be beneficial to you. What is it that God may be
trying to do for you in your next?

You must trust that whatever it is that surely God is going to blow
your mind, especially if He has already shown you.

What are you willing to sacrifice to move forward? Who are you
willing to give up? Are you willing to give up everything for something new?

Change is inevitable, but you must also go about change the right way. You do not want to leave your old lifestyle, friends, and loved ones in a bad manner, but you want to leave with integrity. How will you do this? What will you say and do to ensure that as you move you are moving with integrity and not with a sense of pride or entitlement?

New territory often means a new lifestyle, new friends, being away from loved ones, and of course, new trials and tribulations. You are going to a place that you have never gone before and experiencing things you have never experienced. You will have to do some things differently and be okay with things not being as they once were.

As you embrace the new, it is important to stay prayerful and allow God to guide you daily.

JOURNAL YOUR THOUGHTS

In this new season I am expecting:

_____

_____

_____

_____

_____

_____

_____

_____

_____

_____

_____

_____

_____

_____

JOURNAL YOUR THOUGHTS

How will things change for me when I embrace the new?

_____

_____

_____

_____

_____

_____

_____

_____

_____

_____

_____

_____

_____

JOURNAL YOUR THOUGHTS

**Before I enter this new season, I must
make the following preparations:**

_____

_____

_____

_____

_____

_____

_____

_____

_____

_____

_____

_____

_____

_____

JOURNAL YOUR THOUGHTS

**What old doors do I need to close and
how can I close with integrity?**

_____

_____

_____

_____

_____

_____

_____

_____

_____

_____

_____

_____

_____

JOURNAL YOUR THOUGHTS

What can I say or do to encourage others during my transition?

_____

_____

_____

_____

_____

_____

_____

_____

_____

_____

_____

_____

_____

JOURNAL YOUR THOUGHTS

What am I willing to give up to obey God?

_____

_____

_____

_____

_____

_____

_____

_____

_____

_____

_____

_____

_____

_____

HAVING CONFIDENCE IN TAKING NEW TERRITORY

"Trust in the LORD with all thine heart; and
lean not unto thine own understanding.
In all thy ways acknowledge Him, and He
shall direct thy paths." – Proverbs 3:5-6

*H*aving confidence in God is one of the best things you can possess in this lifetime. Confidence in knowing that He does all things well. Confidence in knowing that He will not lead you astray. Confidence in knowing that even though it does not look good now, it is working for your good.

One way to increase your confidence is to increase your faith. What are some things that are standing in the way of your faith and confidence in God? Do you allow what you see and feel right now to dictate what you feel God can do for you? If so, it is time to change your mindset and allow God to show himself to you. When you begin to doubt, speak the Word over your life. Ask God to reaffirm who He is to you.

As you increase your confidence, you must know that you are unique and special to God. It is okay to be yourself and to walk confidently in knowing who you are. God did not create you like anyone else; therefore, you cannot compare yourself to them nor think that their journey should be your journey.

Speak to God about your fears and expectations. Speak His Word over your life. Because He is the author and finisher of your faith. You must be comfortable in knowing that you are on the right path and set a plan in place to build your confidence and overcome that which is holding you back.

As you move into new territory, confidence is a necessity so that you can tackle everything that is about to come your way. You must be confident in your decisions, your actions, and in your destiny. Are there areas in your life in which you could use a little more confidence? Let God use you and exercise your faith as you move forward.

JOURNAL YOUR THOUGHTS

**What are some words I can say to God
daily? (write a daily prayer)**

_____

_____

_____

_____

_____

_____

_____

_____

_____

_____

_____

_____

_____

JOURNAL YOUR THOUGHTS

What is my plan for transition and taking new territory?

_____

_____

_____

_____

_____

_____

_____

_____

_____

_____

_____

_____

JOURNAL YOUR THOUGHTS

What are some things I can do to increase my confidence?

_____

_____

_____

_____

_____

_____

_____

_____

_____

_____

_____

_____

_____

_____

JOURNAL YOUR THOUGHTS

Things that make me confident are:

_____

_____

_____

_____

_____

_____

_____

_____

_____

_____

_____

_____

_____

_____

JOURNAL YOUR THOUGHTS

God reaffirms Himself to me by:

_____

_____

_____

_____

_____

_____

_____

_____

_____

_____

_____

_____

_____

JOURNAL YOUR THOUGHTS

Who does the Bible say that I am?

_____

_____

_____

_____

_____

_____

_____

_____

_____

_____

_____

_____

_____

Trusting That You Are Not in Trouble During Transition

"The Lord shall preserve thee from all evil: he shall preserve thy soul. The Lord shall preserve thy going out and thy coming in from this time forth, and even for evermore." – Psalm 121:7-8

*P*salm 23 assures us that God is our protector. When going through transition, it is not God's desire that we face trouble; however, trouble can arise as we become disobedient.

We are often disobedient in transition because it may make us feel uneasy and doubt ourselves. It is up to you how you handle and learn from each experience as they can serve as steppingstones to your next level.

Even when it may look like trouble, you are not in trouble because God's Word assures us that we are protected. When you are in tune with the voice of God and understand that His will is that you prosper, you can be assured that you are not in trouble, you are just in transition. Embrace the change and TRUST GOD!!

<u>What the Bible Says About Times of Trouble:</u>

"God is our refuge and strength, a very present help in trouble." – Psalm 46:1

"The name of the Lord is a strong tower: the righteous runneth into it, and is safe." – Proverbs 18:10

"Let not your heart be troubled: ye believe in God, believe also in me." – John 14:1

"The righteous cry, and the Lord heareth, and delivereth them out of all their troubles. The Lord is nigh unto them that are of a broken heart; and saveth such as be of a contrite spirit. Many are the afflictions of the righteous: but the Lord delivereth him out of them all." – Psalm 34:17-19

"For our light affliction, which is but for a moment, worketh for us a far more exceeding and eternal weight of glory." – 2 Corinthians 4:17

JOURNAL YOUR THOUGHTS

What has God shown or said to assure
me that I am not in trouble?

_____

_____

_____

_____

_____

_____

_____

_____

_____

_____

_____

_____

_____

JOURNAL YOUR THOUGHTS

Why does God have me in transition?

_____

_____

_____

_____

_____

_____

_____

_____

_____

_____

_____

_____

_____

JOURNAL YOUR THOUGHTS

What can I do to close my ears to negative voices?

_____

_____

_____

_____

_____

_____

_____

_____

_____

_____

_____

_____

_____

JOURNAL YOUR THOUGHTS

How can I be honest with myself about transition?

_____

_____

_____

_____

_____

_____

_____

_____

_____

_____

_____

_____

_____

JOURNAL YOUR THOUGHTS

When I allowed someone to talk me out of what God said, I felt:

_____

_____

_____

_____

_____

_____

_____

_____

_____

_____

_____

_____

_____

JOURNAL YOUR THOUGHTS

What does God's Word say about protecting those who trust Him?

_____

_____

_____

_____

_____

_____

_____

_____

_____

_____

_____

_____

CONCLUSION

*O*beying God can often take you on a journey that you never expected. However, as you sit and take the time to reflect on His Word and what He is showing you, it will all make sense.

The Bible says: "And the Lord answered me, and said, Write the vision, and make *it* plain upon tables, that he may run that readeth it." – Habakkuk 2:2

"Write the things which thou hast seen, and the things which are, and the things which shall be hereafter." – Revelation 1:19

Now that you have obeyed the Word and completed this journal, treasure it, pray over it, read it often, and reflect upon its contents. As you continue to obey God in transition, you will begin to see the manifestation of what you have written and trust Him even more.

Heavenly Father,

I pray that You would bless this journal and the contents. I thank You for eyes to see, ears to hear, and for the courage to be obedient. I thank You for being God and for loving me enough to allow me to open myself up enough to write and share what I feel and what You have shown me. I thank You for being the God of a second chance and for covering me during my seasons of transition. I ask that You continue to lead and guide me in the direction that You would have for my life. I pray for protection from negativity. Show me how to deal with those people and situations that do not align with what You have shown me for my life. Give me the strength and courage to overcome any fears, doubts, worries, concerns, or anything that is holding me back from moving where and who You want me to be. Send Your angels of comfort during those times where I may feel lonely and give me direction when I do not know which way to go. I ask that you bless the works of my hands and all that I have poured out into this journal. I pray that it will manifest and that in the end You will get all the glory for my life belongs to You.

In Jesus Name,
Amen

CPSIA information can be obtained
at www.ICGtesting.com
Printed in the USA
BVHW072305070821
613216BV00002B/12